Twelve Quakers and God

by

Quaker Quest

Quaker Quest Pamphlet 1

Published in 2004 in the United Kingdom by Quaker Quest, an outreach project of Hampstead Monthly Meeting, Britain Yearly Meeting of the Religious Society of Friends.

ISBN: 0 9543459 1 6

Preface

In 2003 members of the Quaker Quest team agreed to share their experience of the divine. No one was to see the other contributions until all had been completed.

Each writer has felt the near-impossibility of the task. For as soon as the profoundly personal words were written, they either seemed inadequate or the writer had moved on and could no longer stand by them. Some have retired gracefully. But twelve have allowed their words to stand as evidence of where they had reached when they wrote them.

This pamphlet is an attempt to express what some Quakers at the start of the twenty-first century understand about the heart of their faith. The hope is that this might be of value to those who are beginning to explore the Quaker way.

Introduction

What is God? Who is God? Is God the correct name? Why should I be bothered about God, or whatever? What do I believe?

Quakers would say that these are fascinating and creative questions, but they start from the wrong place. For Quakers, God is not a matter of belief but of experience. They start from their own experience. They take responsibility for themselves, and then honestly, carefully, bravely, joyfully look for the truth. The truth they look for is one they can manifest in their lives, not just discuss.

As humans, we use words to communicate, but words cannot be enough. That is why Quakers do not have a creed, a set of words to show that they belong to the same group. Quakers do have beliefs, as individuals, and they have lots in common. But they do not press their words on others.

Twelve Quakers invite you to join in an exploration. They write from their own experience, in their own words. What they write is a tiny contribution to a view of God, to be added to by readers.

The twelve Quakers were involved in organising *Quaker Quest*, a series of open meetings for people interested in the Quaker way as a spiritual path for today which is simple, radical and contemporary.

Quakers have had an influence for good in society outweighing their small numbers. They are a religious society with Christian roots, inspired by the example of Jesus but learning also from the teachings of many faiths. Their worship is simple, waiting together in silence and stillness. What they see as important is the way you live, how that worship helps you to help others. Seeking after God is not to escape from the world, but to find the power in it.

1

Years ago, at the end of an evening's informal group discussion, I heard myself saying, "Well, with my back against the wall, all I can say is: 'For me God Is'."

Now, nearly forty years later, I find myself saying exactly the same thing. Whether I understand any better what I mean by that statement I sometimes wonder. What I do know is that no matter what questions arise, I find myself responding from the same position. It is a position that has become a part of my reality, a part of my being. At the same time it is not a position I could expect anyone else to hold, for I see each of us as being our own authority, finding our own way. I would say that in some ways I feel I am still at the beginning, that the freshness of discovery can be there every moment of every day.

I was brought up in a home where traditional Christian teaching prevailed. Of course I asked questions, and as life went on I found fewer and fewer satisfactory answers. Like so many others I found myself unable to accept much of what seemed important in the practice of my church. In retrospect I think that for me the external practice hid the truth. Eventually, after some really hard searching, I was confronted with the truth. With the word God.

As a child my understanding of this word was built up from being told that God was everywhere but couldn't be seen. I have to say that I was not given any sense of God being a frightening or punishing figure. Today my sense of God has, I am sure, grown from that early teaching, which both satisfied and puzzled me as a child. Of course there was a time when I thought of God as a kind of person, but that understanding is not mine now, although I respect those who walk hand in hand with a personal God.

My understanding of this reality in my life is very simple. I think of absolute love, of total goodness. Of a power which is beyond and is too great for my complete apprehension, yet is part of me, and of all others. A power that humbles and yet enhances. A power that allows absolute freedom yet is there always, even if sometimes hard to find. The words 'seeker after the truth' are so important to me.

I believe that each of us must find his or her own way, that we must be open to the light, which may mean that we discard long-cherished understandings or make surprising and entrancing discoveries. In my experience, it has been in the most surprising places and from seemingly the most unlikely sources that I find God being revealed. This can be when I truly encounter that of God in another, or in the world, or just suddenly entering my mind. Truth for me is the personal encounter with the Divine, with God. Those times when, in the stillness, all is well. When I am carried on the breath of the spirit.

2

I need God in the same way that I need food, drink and sleep. I am absolutely sure that needing God is an integral part of the human condition, and that some people find it harder than others to accept it. They, in their turn, of course, know that I am deluding myself. I believe in God. David Steindl-Rast has said that God is a name for a reality which cannot be named, and that is the closest definition I have ever encountered for the indefinable. For me, God is a reality. I believe in God because I experience it.

It wasn't always that way for me. I spent about thirty years of my life unsure and angry and in a fog. I think now that I was struggling not to believe. I remember sitting next to a man in a self-help group that I was attending, and finding myself seething with unexpressed anger when he said, "Ego stands for Easing God Out." "How dare you question my ego?" I thought. "I need my ego. My ego has brought me the success I've had."

Yet that encounter must have stirred some truth inside me. Three weeks later I sought the man out and asked him in detail what he meant. I wanted to know how he had come to his view, what practice he was adopting, how he could possibly cope with his life without resorting to the power of self.

He made some simple, perhaps naïve, suggestions. He suggested that humility was a better coping mechanism in life than ego. He told me that I would find it easier to understand my life if I were able to key into an energy that was greater than me. He told me that his life had been changed by some simple practices, and that I could begin to adopt them if I wanted to.

I'm constantly astonished by our capacity to turn unbelief into belief. It is as if we are simply flipping a coin. Certainly, that was how it was for me.

I decided not to worry about defining the power I was trying to align myself with. I resolved to get on my knees as I had when I was a child, and burble quietly. I burbled to the child I had been when I was born, that perfect baby boy. I burbled to the force that gave me life. If I wasn't sure about how to pray to God, I could at least burble to Good, so I did that. Quite quickly, over the next three or four weeks, my life began to change utterly. I was undergoing a religious conversion. And it was a surprisingly simple matter.

I won't dwell on the many ways in which my life was upended, because they really aren't the point. What matters is that I turned to something outside myself and I changed – *but I had to ask to do it.*

It is a strange phenomenon that as we ask to move closer to God, God moves closer to us, and when we move away, God becomes harder and harder to discern. Could it be that this great energy is the quintessence of selflessness, as well as of love and truth and the force for good? Well, yes, I think so. That has certainly been my experience. God became a reality for me only because I asked it to.

As a result of these experiences, I fail utterly to understand the argument that "If there were a God there wouldn't be any wars", or "What's God doing about the famine in Ethiopia?" Surely, it is we who cause these difficulties when we fail to align ourselves to the power of God. It is for us to solve them. And we will, if we collectively acquire the humility to ask.

I have stopped praying to Good now. The God that I pray to is inside me, and outside me. When I ask to touch it, it becomes tangible. When I ask for help, I get it, and never in ways that I expect. When I forget about it, it disappears from view.

At best it is a warmth, a real presence in my life. But it can be a disturbing one, too. Belief in God demands change - constant, demanding and sometimes fundamental change. Often I feel painted into corners, as if I am being forced by God to do things against my will. When I fight these impulses (that ego again!) the result is a feeling of cruel disorientation and a lonely understanding that my will was wrong. When I allow the spirit to guide me against my judgement, I change. There emerges a calm in my life. I stop fighting. I feel completely human again.

3

My experience of God is of a force. It is within me, and outside me, omnipresent in the world. It has been with me since childhood, although it has taken years for me to recognise it and to try to express it, and, especially, to be sensitive and responsive to it. I can go for some time without acknowledging it, but it will not leave me alone. It is a force of light and piercing truth; it is a force of love, compassion and mercy. When the force moves through me, compelling me to act, it will not be denied.

This force can be experienced; it can be felt, and that which I feel, I describe as the voice of God, but it is really more a prodding of God. If I sit in stillness, truly opening myself to the prodding, it can rise up within me. I cannot call it up at will, even with great effort; it comes in its own time and when it will, and when it does I describe it as the grace of God. If I sit in stillness with others, in a worshipping group, it can come to us all as a group. When I am entirely open to this force I describe it, in the words of the first commandment, as 'loving the Lord my God with all my heart and all my mind and all my soul'. The second commandment, 'to love my neighbour as myself', follows automatically.

The force that is God is an absolute ethic: that of the second commandment. It calls upon me to exercise love and mercy and to act justly to my fellow beings. Any form of cruelty or killing, anything which diminishes another, is inimical to God. God is total understanding, and all that is understood must be forgiven. In so far as we live in the light of God, we are forgiving. We can but do our best to live within this ethic.

I cannot envisage this force as anthropomorphic. It has not come to humankind magically into a single body at a single point in history. It is always present, waiting to be recognised, in every precious, unique human being, every child of God. Each of us has the potential to act as a conduit of this force. God does not target me, as an individual, or instruct me personally. The God force is always there in all of us at all times. I experience this as a personal message when the force, the light, breaks through in my heart. This grace of God might be experienced by anyone at any time.

I can feel the force of God's light at unexpected moments: as I walk down the street, as a stranger smiles in a crowd, as I look at the sky. I feel the power of God in the vastness of the universe, in the minuteness of a grain of sand. I experience my life both as brief as the day-lily's and yet as a part of the aeons of history. God is manifest in this relativity of time.

As I give thanks for the measure of God that has been granted to my awareness, I pray that it may continue and that I may not fail to respond as a faithful servant.

4

The Akans of Ghana have a saying: *Obi nkyere akodaa Nyame.* 'You don't have to tell a child that there is God because it already knows'. I suppose that's how I feel – that God *is.*

I feel God as a power to be drawn on and from which to receive strength. Sometimes in my life, when all else has failed, I have prayed for this strength and felt at peace.

When I was a child I heard a story about a missionary in the South Seas who was composing a sermon and was finding it difficult to translate 'trust in God', until a tired visitor arrived, and, sinking down into a chair, said, in the local language: "How good it is to rest my full weight on this seat." There was the translation, and I feel that's how it is.

I can believe in God as an originator of life, the universe, etc, which has been left to evolve, but as for the inventor or the creator of individual species, then – why the cockroach?

5

"Do you believe in God?" is a question I imagine being asked by people like Richard Dawkins, who loves to debate the issue in his wonderful books about evolution. His chosen antagonists seem to be fundamentalists for whom God is a supernatural creator, father, and judge. The question puts me on the defensive. I want to answer: "Well, it depends what you think God is."

That doesn't seem a very good place to start.

Then there's the word 'believe', which seems to denote something asserted in the face of contradictory evidence. Yet we say that Quakerism is experiential. If I have experienced something, I know it; I don't have to 'believe' it.

So I am going to start somewhere else, with Faith. Quakers call their book of guidance and inspiration *Quaker Faith and Practice.* Faith is a word I feel comfortable with. I know I have faith. Faith is what gets me out of bed in the morning and it determines what I do, my practice.

Faith in what?

I say that there is such a thing as 'worth'. That everything is not relative, or expedient. That some things and actions are better than others. I see an endless struggle between forces for good on the one hand and evil and apathy on the other. My faith is not a blind belief that good will overcome evil and despair in the end and that all will be perfect, but rather that good energy will always be there, bringing its blessings, and that I can obtain joy by doing my bit to share those blessings and that love with others.

Faith is about there being meaning in my life, from knowing that I am not just an isolated individual, but part of a whole, and that I have my place and role within that.

The theologian Mary Daly has written, 'Why indeed must "god" be a noun? Why not a verb ... the most active and dynamic of all?' I agree with that. I can live with the term God as energy, force, direction, rather than a thing or a person.

Another metaphor for God is a ball of many mirrored facets. We all see a part of it, and what we see reflects back to us a unique perspective, which is a true reflection yet only part of the whole. In this way, I can accept that others will have a different view of God, different words for God, different experiences of God, and yet all these are but glimpses of fragments of the same thing, which is greater than anything we can comprehend.

These are some of the fragments I see:
Photographs of our precious, tiny, green planet, in the vastness and darkness of space. Surely, we have to stick together and care for one another and our common home, or we are nothing. Some people I know can contemplate the heavens and stars and infinity of space and find solace, strength and inspiration from that. I can't quite get that far yet. My faith is rather earth-bound, even tied to humanity, rather than other forms of life.

Mountains that have the power to take me out of myself, out of the now. I know that mountains are not eternal, but they seem immovable, unperturbed by storms, human settlement and extraction of logs or minerals. In the words of the psalm: 'I raise my eyes unto the hills from whence my help comes.' God is more eternal than mountains.

Great music. Many composers, writers, painters speak of what they create as coming from God through them. I find sacred choral music takes me the closest I get to a sense of awe, wonder, praise and of the tenderness of the divine.

A leaf on a tree. The leaf buds and opens, doing its bit for the growth of the tree, creating oxygen. Then, the leaf withers and dies and falls to the ground, still contributing to the nourishment of the soil, and the tree lives on.

So I have faith that it is worth my doing something. But how to decide what to do? Here I have found Quakers offer a method. To be still enough to listen, and to share and support one another. But who or what am I listening to? Do I hear anything? How do I know that a thought I have is a leading from God?

People ask, "If God is an all-powerful force, then why can't it stop pain and suffering, fear and war?" If God is the energy, then it is trying to stop these things. And if God is in us, then we must be part of the effort to stop them.

I am on a journey, a path that winds around a mountain; I see the same thing from different perspectives all the time. But I know there is a path, that it leads somewhere, and that there is a force that is moving me along it.

6

To define or to describe God is to distort, to impose our own limitations of time and space. I can only give my own experience thus far.

I experience God as the life-force, the spark of the Divine, not dualistically a creator, but immanent: the One manifest in the many. All the richness and variety of the natural world is an expression of God. 'Every creature is a word of God', as the medieval mystic, Meister Eckhart, said. I experience God both in the uniqueness of living creatures - the birdness of a bird, the treeness of a tree - and in that which brings us together: the unifying and connecting principle between and within all creation, the movement in our hearts at the beauty of the natural world, the joy of recognition in the eyes of another human being. God as relationship.

I experience God as Being, unlimited by time or space. Our dream world, sense of *deja vu*, or ecstatic experiences when all seems gathered in a present moment, are intimations of divine eternity, as are the stars, which we see millions of years after they are shown to us.

I experience God as purpose, a purpose in which we participate, in a continuing process of creation, transformation, resurrection and revelation.

I experience God as a presence in my heart and in my bowels, in the depths of my being; in the desert and in the tiniest chapel; in music and dance as well as in the stillness and silence; in joy and anguish, darkness and light. In the indivisibility of God we understand the connectedness of opposites.

God is a guiding force in my life. Until recently I could not feel God as love, but I have come to an understanding recently that the love is in the relationship, the connectedness which I experience consciously through others and, vividly, unexpectedly, through acts of synchronicity. Glimpses of connections that I had not previously understood: connections that show me the way, affirm my steps on the path, nurture me, not with the cuddly limited love of my imaginings, but with the mature love and acceptance of my real self.

Prayer for me is largely a matter of adoration and thankfulness. In terms of the events of my life and that of others, it is rarely petitionary or intercessionary, except in moments of extremity. When facing the foreknowledge of the Divine, only 'Thy Will be Done' seems appropriate. I strive for the state of grace that was expressed by a member of my Quaker Meeting, who said, "I want to thank God for everything, including the things I didn't want."

7

From very young I have been awe-struck by experiences I had no name for. As I grew up I came to understand these in terms of God. Quakers use many words for God – Spirit, the Divine, etc – perhaps because they have associated the word with some, now unacceptable, picture of a vengeful old man in the sky. I have always used God because that is the word with which I am most comfortable. It represents for me in its many translations the way humans have sought to give a name to explain the spiritual and the moral. So I shall use God, and I hope it will not be a barrier for you.

What I have learned is that I experience this God as both closer than breath (and quite alarmingly personal and loving!) and yet also as infinite, creative and unknowable.

I meet this God, often unexpectedly – in joy, in suffering, occasionally in nature, in the most minute particulars of daily life, and often in people. Indeed, it is often in the least likely people that I catch a glimpse of their goodness, their 'Godness'.

I encounter, rather than believe in, God. But I have chosen, and it is a choice, to bet my life (literally) on the power, the love, the challenge, that I call God. For me it has always been a stark choice. You take it seriously (or try to) twenty-four hours a day or not at all. Like pregnancy, there are no half measures – I can no more be 'a little bit religious' than 'a little bit pregnant'!

It is not easy. I go for long periods with grave doubt. There was at least one time in my life when I was not just agnostic but quite sure that there was no God. 'Life's a bitch and then you die' seemed to me to be the most realistic assessment of everything. But somehow, so far, I haven't cancelled the bet.

There are those who will feel that the sum of the divine sparks in everyone is all that any God can be; for others, the divine they encounter is a power but seems unlikely to have anything to do with the creation and sustaining of the universe. I'm probably amongst those who suspect that the God I encounter is even more than the creator and sustainer.

I am always mindful of the old story of the blind men describing the elephant. One holds the tail and suggests the animal is like a rope, another feels the side and says it is more like a wall. One holding the leg says it must be a tree, while another at the trunk insists on it resembling a snake. Can we ever really know all of the nature of God?

This is expressed well in a complex Hindu concept – *sarvadharmasambhava.* This says that as a result of one's own experience of the ultimate we may be able to understand a similar experience of another and respect it. But from this deep experience of ultimateness and universality at the depth of one's own religious faith what results is not a superficial suggestion that 'all religions are the same', but a capacity to understand that the experience of another may be equally ultimate and universal but quite different from one's own. We may recognise the validity of the encounter yet not recognize the God of whom the other speaks. This is a religious tolerance based on a deep respect, 'the homage which the finite mind pays to the inexhaustibility of the infinite,' in the words of Radhakrishnan.

I think this is very important to remember. And yet, and yet... There is a paradox. When I speak with my friend who is a devout Muslim, we find that as we talk of our lives and our work, as we move beyond the words to the spaces in between them and truly let those moments of attentiveness to each other address us, so we find a deep unity in our encounter with God ('closer than our jugular vein', as the Koran says).

And it is in that hospitality of listening and waiting that we Quakers can find our unity with one another amidst the very different words we use.

8

'The song of the Spirit is everywhere': its melody resonates throughout my experience and its lyric haunts my attempts at understanding.

This *experience* of the divine comes to me unexpectedly in flashes, sudden openings, when the penny drops, or things click into place. This is a glimpse of the other, 'rumours of angels', a tangential glancing blow of the holy. No Damascus visions or burning bushes, but humble occasions which I recognise, often long afterwards, as times of inner enlargement when my own spirit has magnified or manifested something greater.

The ground-swell burden of these Spirit experiences rises from the heart of the caring and loving I have known from being a much-wanted child and a well-accepted partner in a merry marriage. From profound family illnesses and the deaths of parents, sister and friends to the anxieties and joys of the births of children and grandchildren there have been myriad times when I have touched the transcendent in laughter and loneliness, in the sensualities of the flesh and the companionship of loved ones, in breakdown and breakthrough. And so I learned to trust life and to feel that I belonged.

The tunes in counterpoint sing of a presence evoked through beauty and fear, in meadow and mountain, as child and teenager, birdwatching or camping under radiant stars, awe and wonder palpable. They echo from transformations in the absorption of play at any age when time stands still and my ego is lost in another medium - music, film, books or theatre-making. They resonate out of the stillness of worship following a deep experience by a now opened and bonded group.

But most revealing of the nature of the Spirit are those times of despair and hurt and meaninglessness, when life, I believed, was being unfair to me, or when the world, I felt, was grossly unjust and tragic to others, and I have needed to surrender myself to the creative powers within to heal and to reconcile or to lead me into new insights and new ways. This Power does not step in 'over there', to intervene in calamity or holocaust, but it does melt a new pathway 'in here', within myself.

I have found that my *understandings* of the song of the Spirit change my experiences, and these then call for new understandings. Just as the gods no longer speak through the thunderclouds now that we know of thermal air currents, so the concept of God no longer speaks to me at all. I cannot separate the word God from an anthropomorphic being, whether judge or father, lord or king, with a will that may be determined and known rather than a way of free choice.

So I lay down God as noun and take up the Spirit as verb - an eternal process, that is evolving and creative, genuinely open, free and without destination. For the Spirit itself evolves as the universe and humanity evolve; our spiritual quest is a story of new revelations. Experiencing this power of Spirit has been real for me, not a linguistic metaphor, so I look for a realistic understanding.

I read of the beginnings of the universe emanating from a point of singularity, like an exhalation from another state beyond our universe's dimensions, a quantum plenum full of infinite potential. In less than a split second an explosion of quantum riches expanded into a quantum energy field out of which all that is material has come and where, after its transitory manifestation as galaxy, star, dolphin or philosopher, will ultimately return. We are temporary negotiations of this final Truth: all is of the Spirit and in the Spirit; transcendence is shot through the immanent. This energy field is my divinity, the oneness and wholeness of all; matter *is* energy. I recognise it as sacred, so each of its expressions in our universe is sacred.

As energy resonating with the consciousness of our minds, which have evolved as its receptors, the Spirit is ultimately unknowable because it is chaotic and uncertain. But as matter, out of which humanity has been fashioned, it is eminently knowable through all our varieties of discourse. The prophet, artist, scientist and mystic equally reveal its principles, just as cancer, AIDs, penicillin and aspirin reveal the variety of its contingency. The Spirit knows no chosen people; everyone is a unique, experimental expression of the divine, regardless of gender or colour or sexual orientation.

The Spirit is more than love, but it cannot be caged in dogma and creed. Yet I need a belief to live by which gives meaning and focus. When I am aligned to the way of the Spirit's freedom and in harmony with its principles then growth is healthy and true, not to be made perfect but to be fulfilled in my uniqueness. The soul, the heart, the light, the Christ, the seed are each universal notions of the source of this growth. I cannot escape from the embrace of the Spirit within me and all about me. My pride and self-centeredness can block it out, but it is there waiting; its song resonates through me until I finally become one with it again.

9

In my life experience the Divine has been a reality. The God of love, compassion and tender upholding is one that I have known. But my God is not just personal; S/he is also power or energy, the Divine Source. This Divine Power is part of all creative energy, which cannot be defined or confined, just glimpsed in creation and creative forms. It is a mystical Other, in which and with which I am engaged. Jesus was someone who more clearly knew this Divine Spirit than most, and lived his life in joyful response to it.

The spiritual path towards awareness of the Divine is not one which is found through guilt, duty or conformity; rather it is known in the joy-filled wholeness of the full reality of life. This Divine Spirit, however, can invade my orderliness and jolt me; it pushes out the comfortable boundaries; it demands that I struggle to be in balance with it; it requires my response.

As we are all part of this known and unknown Divine Energy, so we are in relation to all others and to all created things; my self and my actions directly affect all else, so I am therefore an integrated part of the universal whole.

I believe that the power of prayer with God can bring about change, usually in subtle and longer-term ways, but sometimes in the immediate. I can also be transformed and changed by others' encounters with God, and also in what they write.

So, at the moment, my God finds expression in:
The joy of *The God of Surprises,*
The affirmation of *The Cloud of Unknowing;*
The comfort of Julian of Norwich in *A Revelation of Love*
The awe of Thomas Kelly's *The Testament of Devotion*
and the wonder of *The Coming of the Cosmic Christ.*

But this is an exploration, a journey; and how on this spiritual path may I yet come to know the Divine?

10

I have never really been sure about God. Throughout my childhood I really can't remember believing in God, but didn't positively disbelieve either. At school we sang hymns, and the only ones I remember being at all moved by were the ones about nature, particularly one that talks about the stars appearing in the evening, showing

> 'myriad worlds unknown;
> and man, the marvel seeing
> forgets his selfish being
> for joy of beauty not his own.'

The sexist language didn't bother me back then, and even now this verse speaks to me. My Quaker parents encouraged me to look at the words of the hymns critically and decide for myself what I could accept.

I remember, perhaps as a student, formulating my belief like this: some impulse in me sometimes leads me to be generous, or unselfish, and other people talk about being led by God to this kind of goodness, so I might as well call the impulse I feel God as well.

I have always liked to spend time outdoors, especially on my own, and used to sit at the top of an apple tree, from where I could see the hills in the distance. I sometimes got an inspired kind of feeling in places like this, and still do, and this feeling seems to fit with other experiences that people call spiritual or religious or of God. It is a similar feeling to being deeply moved, for example by hearing someone's personal story or by a work of art or music, and I choose to call this feeling spiritual as well.

Sometimes I think I am verging on being atheist, because I think it is quite possible that the inspiring and leading God I believe in could be a product of my mind (and the minds of other people). The human brain is such a marvellous thing, full of mystery, that I don't think it is a problem to find one more mystery in it. But God may equally be outside us all – I really don't know. I don't spend much time worrying about theology - it is the inspiration and the impetus to change the world for the better that really matter.

One aspect that some people apply to God is one I have a problem with: the creator. I studied biology in order to find out more about how the wonderful world works, and the more I learnt about the evolution of life, the more wonderful I found it. But this wasn't wonder at what the divine creator had made, but an amazement that all this beauty and complexity can come about by entirely understandable processes, without outside intervention.

As a scientist I prefer rational explanations for things, if such explanations exist. Also, I don't think that believing in a creator God would help me in my life, whereas the inspiration and direction I get from the other aspects of the divine are very helpful indeed. The idea of Mother Earth doesn't appeal to me either - it seems too simplistic to reduce the whole earth to one human-like character.

Strangely enough, I don't find the concept of God as either father or mother helpful very often, though occasionally I find myself needing to pray to a kind of parent figure. Once recently I found myself saying 'Lord' when I wanted to talk to the divine, which seemed odd given the patriarchal overtones of the word. But these days one hardly hears the word Lord in any context except for that of God, whereas the word God itself is over-used ('Oh, my God' is a phrase I use far too much, in a non-spiritual way).

One place where I feel God most strongly is in Quaker meetings for worship. In business meetings especially, which are based on silent waiting for God's leadings, I have felt the group being drawn to the best decision even when I or others strongly disagreed.

11

I am distressed when I read of yet another war about God's name, somewhere in God's world. What pain, what unimaginable grief the Creator must feel at this perversion of the Creation.

I use many names for the Divine, sometimes lingering with one sacred name, but wary of becoming territorial, my god shrinking to mere possession. Early Quakers used Light, giving life and clarity, showing me the next steps, and Light is probably the word I use most of all.

In the Bible I do like God as mother hen sheltering her young, God as artisan, delighting in Wisdom (who is also

God, and female), playing by God's side from the beginning of creation. John's gospel sees Wisdom as Jesus. Each word suggests different manifestations. When I was pregnant, the babyhood of God gave me hope and promise.

My experience is that God is beyond all our imagining, bigger than any one name we humans use. Dios, Gott, El, Yahweh, Allah, Ahura Mazda – I could never learn enough languages to pronounce all the names of God; I cannot in this life explore all these understandings.

I want to express my awe before the greatness of God, but have not – yet – found the vocabulary. I was not brought up in a country with a monarch, and cannot find any reality in Lord. Some cannot bear God as father or mother, for only cruelty and betrayal come to mind; perhaps those who have suffered need Friend, Comforter, Healer. Ground of Being, or Truth to me feel cold and abstract, yet feel warm to others – how wonderfully odd!

The early Quaker, George Fox, could have been speaking for me, when he said:

> 'Now where is this spirit, and where is this truth? Is it not within people?... And so every man and woman in the whole world must come to the spirit and truth in their own hearts, by which they must know the God of truth.'

The words of Samuel Fisher, another early Quaker, excite me (though I would not use 'he' or 'she'):

> 'Ye query, what God really is in himself?... God, as he is really in himself, is beyond all definition of ours at all.'

Beyond definition, yes, but there are limitations to my inclusive approach. I cannot accept the Maya and Aztec god, who demanded human sacrifice, the living hearts torn from captives and from their own children, offered daily to ensure the world did not end. I have difficulty even learning from this view of God. My approach to God is universal, but I realise some gods are not-God. I have to discriminate. The God I find to be real and whom I worship is just, loving, ethical, and much, much more, but not capricious or cruel.

This has turned into a love song to the One Who is my Life and my End (God is clearly Capital Letters too!).

12

What I worship, what is divine for me, is the fundamental Energy of on-going creation with its millions of worlds and trillions of beings. Through infinite time it is leading us towards a Consciousness when all things will share the same Mind.

Humanity is a speck of dust in all this, but as one amid the many I try to sense the direction of Consciousness and to live in response to it. That is our purpose. In any context we can each respond in ways that are more or less in line with it, with the spirit of it, the closer alignment elevating the 'spirit in which we live'.

One response is to be in awe of the sheer diversity from molecule to universe and of every expression of the Life-Force. Another is to celebrate progress towards fulfilling Life's potential, including the developments of consciousness of self, of love and the ability to sacrifice self for that which is divine.

But these were not my first responses. Those were to respond to the love of those around me, and then to the teaching of Jesus about love and his expression of it. I saw its potential and experienced its life-enhancing power as I opened myself up to allow love to pass through me. Touched, humbled but elevated, not understanding or needing any explanation, from then I've worked out the implications in service, alive (in varying degrees) to the Energy around and within.

The ever-present Energy is there to be drawn on by anyone who opens himself or herself to it. It calls us in the direction of love and compassion, understanding and forgiveness, and whatever else supports the unity of Life, from social inclusion on local and global scales to care of the natural environment. Opening yourself up is challenging, a direction which is in tension with the opposite drive to control your life, protect and enhance your position and become less vulnerable.

When I trust the relationship with the Energy, I can take risks and grow in faith. I try to develop my Consciousness through silent attention to it in a Quaker Meeting, open to inspiration and in company with others, as well as through reading and reflection. This I find helpful in enabling me to respond to the divine, especially as reflected in others, though my weakness is greater than my strength.

Recommended reading:

Quaker Faith and Practice: the book of Christian discipline of the Yearly Meeting of the Religious Society of Friends (Quakers) in Britain. London: Britain Yearly Meeting, 2nd edition, 1999

Grubb, Martyn: *Truth and God:* one person's experience. London: Quaker Home Service, 1989

Kelly, Thomas R.: *A testament of devotion.* London: Quaker Home Service, 1979

Lacout, Pierre: *God is silence.* London, Quaker Books, pocket edition, 1993

Punshon, John: *Encounter with silence:* reflections from the Quaker tradition. London: Quaker Home Service, 1987

This pamphlet and all of the books listed above are available from:

The Quaker Bookshop
Friends House
173-7 Euston Road
London NW1 2BJ
020 7663 1030/31